GAMESTOP
PHENOMENON

WHEN MONEY MOVES

MICHAEL STANKO

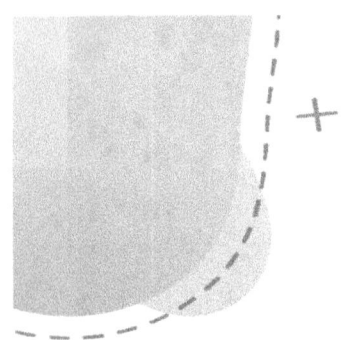

Disclaimer

All rights to this book are reserved. No permission is given for any part of this book to be reproduced, transmitted in any form or means; electronic or mechanical, stored in a retrieval system, photocopied, recorded, scanned, or otherwise. Any of these actions requires the proper written permission of the author.

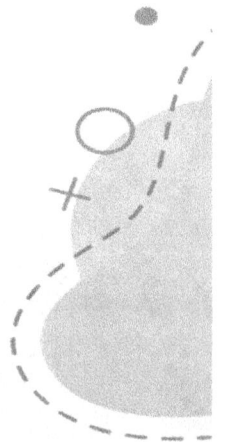

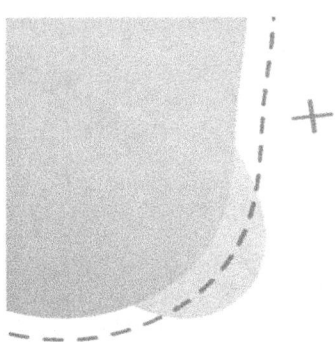

All Right Reserved

All knowledge contained in this book is given for informational and educational purposes only. The author is not in any way accountable for any results or outcomes that emanate from using this material. Constructive attempts have been made to provide information that is both accurate and effective, but the author is not bound for the accuracy or use/misuse of this information.

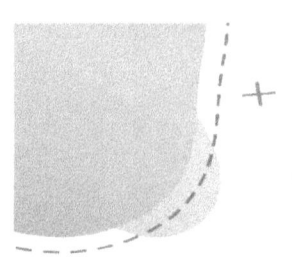

Table Of Contents

Introduction	01
The GameStop Phenomenon	09
Understanding The Stock Market	17
Active Trading and Common Strategies	24
Beginning Your Trade Journey	31
The Indicators	36
Tips to Make a Successful Investment	45

01 Introduction

Every one of us aims to become successful and achieve whatever we wish in our lives. What do you think makes a person successful? Although there is substantial evidence that several factors affect your success, a majority of people believe that money is the most important, if not the only, parameter that determines your success, the more money you have, the more successful you are.

People around the world spend 16 years of their beautiful life learning what would help them earn, while the next 46 in compiling fortune for what they wish to have, and then finally, a small portion of their life in spending what they earned when they were full of life. Money might not buy happiness, but it has all that you need to bring you the latest Rolls Royce or the finest mansion, which might not only attract pleasure but satisfaction.

Earning money isn't a challenging job after all, for all you need is a mind that is looking after ways to earn. Undoubtedly, The world is filled with opportunities, but none of them are going to knock at your door by themselves. Each of them will stay in the room until you get up from your comfort zone and raise your hand to tap the door. The door might not open at the first attempt, but repeated attempts shall bring successful results.

There are numerous ways to get rich; some would say you need to save for the rest of your life, while others would say that you need to invest all you have; but both these measures have their limitations. For the former, if you were to spend your entire life saving for the future, when are you going to spend it, probably on your funeral. Similarly, the latter puts you at enormous risk, which can, in dire cases, leave you in a worse condition than you would have been in without investing.

The most optimal way is to create a balance between both the methods to suit your lifestyle and risk-taking ability. Many experts have recommended that "amassing wealth should be based on current savings and present investments rather than past savings and future investments." The results of your investments shouldn't be on long-term potential but on a monthly rise basis, and your investment should not be coming from money that you have kept in the bank for a long time instead by reducing your present-day expenditures.

03

The simplest way, to begin with, is by saving 40% of your entire monthly income and investing it on 1% returns per month. Let's suppose Mr. X earns $2500 monthly while Mr. Y earns a whopping $50,000, but Mr. X decides to stick to our theory while Mr. Y believes in spending everything that he has rather than saving for a better future. The 40% of Mr. X's salary is 100 dollars which are to be invested at 1% returns in any business or bank, which means a return of 1 dollar in the first month. The overall savings for the two months would be 203.1 dollars; for the first six months period, it would be approximately $700, which ain't even comparable to Mr. Y's monthly earning. Things start to get interesting as soon as the time begins increasing, by the end of year 1, Mr. X is expected to have approximately $2000 in his bank account, by the end of year 2, the amount would rise six times to roughly $12000, as soon as we approach the end of year 3, the amount would be as enormous as $36000, and by the end of year 5, the little saving with just 1% return would turn into a vast fortune of approximately $180,000, which is far more than anything Mr. Y would have in his backup. "A penny saved is a penny earned, but a penny saved and

invested is two pennies earned," you can see how a consistent investment of just $6000 overall could bring tremendous results.

Thanks to the motivational speakers around, people are often aware of the benefits of spending less and investing more, but what puts them in a perplexed state is where to invest? There are a few streams that can turn into a good source of returns, but the drawbacks come with them.

The first option is to keep your money in a fixed bank deposit over monthly returns, and your investment stays safe. The method would work out most times as the interests are well over our benchmark of 1%, and there is no risk involved regarding losing your investment. However, it has certain limitations, such as you won't be paid any interest if you withdraw your investment halfway through; similarly, most saving deposits last for more than five years, which means that you can't have your investment back until the end of the period if you wish to keep the returns.

The second option is to become an entrepreneur by investing in your startup. Everyone knows how a startup can be a game-changer for them; it could bring piles and piles of wealth while there is a fair chance that it could leave you under severe bankruptcy.

Many people tend to go for the startup option and put most of their savings into it, but the latest researches don't show bright prospects. According to studies, 50% of the businesses that began their operations in 2014 had to shut down by the end of 2019, while 50% of the failures didn't even last a year. The count of businesses that failed is as high as 350,000, a number large enough to pursue you towards another alternative.

The third option is to invest in a business that is already set up; it can either be in the form of partnership or purchasing stocks. Partnerships refer to pairing up with another entrepreneur in sharing the responsibility, ownership, and profits of a firm. It is often an excellent choice to go for businesses that are running smooth and have good profitability, as you won't have to worry much about losing the investments. However, partnerships have often experienced losses in the long run as partners wish to escape responsibilities and transfer more jobs to each other while having equal shares; this embeds anger and dislikeliness in their hearts which leads to losses in the long run, in some instances, partners are often found to cheat each other and run away with the investments. Along with it, the partnerships are considered as unincorporated businesses thus have limited liabilities, which means that in case the business fails, any existing debts would have to be paid by the owner's personal fortune.

The next alternative is to purchase shares, more commonly known as stocks, of a publicly listed company, which gives you a share of the ownership of the company and entitles you to a dividend, a share of the profit. However, the primary source of earning through stocks isn't by waiting for dividends but by trading shares on a consistent basis, buying shares when they are low, and selling as they get higher. Stock markets had seen a rise in investments worldwide, mainly due to Covid cutbacks. Many educated professionals were made unemployed, and the stock market, which is a reliable source of earning, was one of the rivers in which investments flowed with no bounds.

The stock market is a funny and equally dangerous business; for anyone that is a spectator, they would always see the investment as high uncertainty and little returns if we consider the dividends only. The perception is true to some extent, as the stock market behaves rigorously at certain times, and the profit and losses can be huge, massive enough to change the value of your fortunes within a day.

To quote an example, Byco from KSE-100(Karachi stock exchange) had an 18.78% rise on the market closing while at the next day closing, the value had a steep fall of 20.3%, which means for someone who owned the share the first day and kept them till the end of the next day would have a net loss of approximately 2%. However, it isn't big to think that the loss would have been bothering, but think of investors who sold their shares after the first day's rise, or of investors who bought it seeing the increase on the first day. One had an increase that was big enough for any other business to replicate in a day, while the latter had a fall which no other firm would commonly suffer. The stock market is a lot more than gambling your money, which many spectators may conceive; it is based on investing in the real-time business and succeeding or falling with them; it isn't based on assuming which company would do big instead critically analyzing what possible company would have better profitability based upon their decisions.

The market undeniably works as per market news and rumors; for instance, if the news is fabricated regarding a business's venture with a foreign company, the share prices are bound to rise the next day as the investors anticipate it to grow, and as soon as, the news turns out to be false, the investors might switch their investors hurriedly, which might lead to a rapid decline.

A famous event that bought the walls street in the main news again lately is an interesting one. The GameStop phenomenon, as most pundits label it, became one of the most discussed stock market events on the news and social media sites, mainly Reddit. The event was an exact replication of how the stock market may behave and depicted us the strengthened force of communication that social media has become. In this book, we shall discuss everything that shall help you get started in the stock exchange, from a summary about its components to detailed analysis on the indicators, the tips to succeed in the market, and of course, everything about the GameStop phenomenon.

09 The GameStop Phenomena

Take yourself back to March 2020 and think of all the uncertainty and problems that surrounded you; the coronavirus pandemic had already started to create an impact during the period, the businesses were closing down, people were being made unemployed, inflation was rising, and economic conditions deteriorating. Many businesses, including the larger companies, had to face huge losses, and cutbacks were made; the wall street NY during the period moved in a similar fashion, investors started driving out their money which resulted in high supply of share and low demand; it led to a market disequilibrium thus the share value fell exponentially. Companies such as Airbnb had the greatest net worth decline in the history of their existence.

However, there were certain companies that flourished too; for instance, the shares of Amazon had a significant rise which was well illustrated by the immense increase in the net worth of its co-owner, Jeff Bezos. The net worth of Mr. Bezos rose to the highest for anyone in history; he became the first person in history to cross the landmark of $200 billion as the share value grew.

10

Despite the tremendous rise in Amazon's share value, it should not be assumed to be the basis of the larger share of the market, mainly for two reasons. Firstly, Amazon is a big business that has worldwide operations and fame, which means that it had lesser chances of failure compared to a regular business that operates in Europe only. Secondly, it had most, if not all, of its significant operations online; having a virtual business setup allowed Amazon to operate effectively during the lockdown. The customers were able to order everything they wished from their phones thus had no physical connection. This, instead, allowed Amazon to overtake a newer market of consumers who prefer to purchase the product through physical markets. As all the relevant markets were closed, these consumers had to shift online and make a purchase through websites, thus easing the roads for Amazon while making it equally challenging for the competitors.

One such business which was apprehended to have a steep fall in its share value was GameStop, an American gaming shop, consumer electronics, and merchandise store, it began in the year 1984 and employed around 22000 full-time employees while

44000 part-time workers in 2019, it has several stores around America, but the flagship store is located in Dallas, Texas.

The gaming store had the primary product as games for consoles, the sales of the store observed a gradual decline in the past few years mainly because of additional competition and lack of demand of games through stores. Most of the games can now be downloaded from the respective app stores of the consoles, and the payments could be made through any card; therefore, the demand for physical CDs and DVDs saw a gradual decline.

Similarly, the fashion of online shopping has peaked during the last decade, and people are no longer reluctant to try online shopping without the fear of being scammed; kids also prefer to opt for online shopping, as buying it directly from the official website allows a free trial for a certain period which helps them make a better purchase. Precisely from all the above discussion, you can assume that the GameStop was dying and the covid was probably the last nail in its coffin, but your assumption is wrong there, as the company rose amongst the ranks to be one of the fortune 500 company, surprising right?

12

It was equally surprising for all the investors and experts out there too because the company didn't have a rise because of its internal policymaking or its profitability, but due to an external factor, the revenge from the big investors that were responsible for the 2008 crash and all the losses that incurred during it. It was a wave of share purchases that began from a Reddit post and took the company to an all-time high value. We shall discuss the event in detail but let's first learn about shorting and its examples as it shall be helpful in our discussion ahead.

Shorting is a concept that is specifically related to the larger stock markets, and several large groups of investors have been utilizing it to make massive profits in a falling market.

In simple terms, shorting means to sell a share before acquiring them and then making the delivery at a later date; the concept gets tricky to understand, so let's take an example of currency exchange.

For instance, you have received secret news that America is going to amend its foreign policy, which would result in the depreciation of the dollar in the world trade. Now your next move would definitely be to sell any dollars you have, but In our example, you have none, so at this moment, you can neither buy any more dollars as they are going to depreciate nor sell it, but what you can do is "shorting." You find a buyer for the dollars and pursue him to make a contract as per the dollar price for the day but delivery for tomorrow. Let's assume that the dollar was worth 100 INR, and its depreciation cause it to fall to 95 INR, which means that you had a profit of 5 INRs.

However, things don't always go as we plan them to, and news can possibly turn out to be rumors only; let's believe that your perception backfired, and instead of depreciating the dollar appreciated to 110 INR, this means that you would be getting 100 INRs while you would have to pay dollars equivalent of 110 INRs, a direct loss of 10 INRs. This was a simple example of shorting, which gets tricky as we enter the share market; it can be taken as a form of gambling where investors put their money with the expectation of the share falling. If the share falls, they win if it appreciates, they lose.

The GameStop phenomenon became a famous example of shorting backfire; as we have discussed above, the sales of GameStop were falling, and the pandemic followed by lockdown made things worse.

14

It could be anticipated the share prices would have a steep fall; many investors thought the same too. Investors at the Wallstreet often bet about how shares would react and make the shorting moves.

As it was anticipated that the GameStop would fall in the latter days, investors started short selling it in large quantities, trading shares worth huge investments. The short-selling patterns don't often leak, which results in losses for the general public, but this time the luck wasn't easy on the investors, and the news broke out on Reddit.

A social media user posted that he had confirmed the news that investors had short sold GameStop shares in the market, and it would possibly decline sharply in coming days, which would bring considerable profits to the "cunning" investors while massive losses for the "innocent" public; the post had a tone of resentment and revenge as it accused these investors of the enormous losses in 2008 crash, and mentioned that it was the "our time to take the revenge."

The post was strong enough to erupt a wave of emotional responses, and people started buying the shares of GameStop, the increase in demand of the share rose its value immensely, and it soon became a surprising addition to the list of market gainers.

15

Its name on the list caught the attention of Elon Musk, a person who is famous for moving the stock market with his tweets. For example, in 2020, Mr. Musk tweeted about tentative and unconfirmed future plans for Tesla, which led to a sudden and massive fall in its share value; the same happened for GameStop but in the opposite manner.

Elon Musk posted a tweet writing "GameStop (two emojis)," the tweet had a link attached which directed to an article regarding its sharp rise in value. Things went as one would expect them to; people started investing massively in GameStop, the demand rose so high that the value of share increased from USD 11.57 on 18th Nov 2020 to USD 347.51 on 27th Jan 2021, it was one of the greatest rises in the history of walls street, the value of the share sat on the same table as Amazon, Tesla, and other major brands; it became one of the Fortune 500 companies out of nowhere. The rise of the share was approximately 2900% to its original value; the shareholders of the company enjoyed huge profits while the short sellers suffered from massive losses.

16

The GameStop phenomenon was an example of money movement in the stock market, one good decision, one relevant post, and a slight Elon Musk hint, and the shares of the company can skyrocket or have a severe ground burial. There is a lot more about the stock market, which this book shall teach you; once you know the certainty and luck involved, it's time that we get into more technical details such as indicators so that you are set to earn through the stock market.

17. Understanding The Stock Market

Every product has a designated market, where buyers and sellers meet, interact, and trade. For instance, people go to the local timber market to buy wood and other necessary material required for home furniture and renovations. Such platforms or designated markets enable buyers to get their desired commodity or product at a fair price while allowing the sellers to meet and trade with a vast number of potential buyers who are interested in purchasing that product or service. Along with it, these designated market or platforms creates competition among different buyers. Thus, enabling them to sell their products at a competitive price. For instance, if there is only one timber seller in the entire town, the seller will have the freedom to charge as he knows there isn't another seller in the entire city. However, if the number of wood sellers is significant in a marketplace, they will have to compete against each other to attract buyers.

Similarly, a stock market is a designated platform where numerous securities are traded in a controlled and secured way. The platform has a vast audience that wants to trade their stocks. A massive market of buyers and sellers ensures transparency and fairness. In the beginning, the stocks were issued in the form of paper-based certificates, but now it's operated through computers electronically. Thus, ensuring fairness and transparency.

The concept behind the stock market's operation is relatively straightforward, and it operates just like an auction house, where the buyers and sellers negotiate and transact. You may have previously heard about the Stock Exchange Markets such as London Stock Exchange, New York Stock Exchange, or Nasdaq. These Stock Exchange Market act as a platform where buyers purchase stocks from the sellers.

In a stock exchange market, companies or business issues their stocks, and sell them to the general public for the first time by the process of Initial Public Offering (IPO). Once the Stocks of a business or a company are listed on the stock exchange market, the investors can buy and invest in that business or company. This helps companies generate capital from the investors, which the business can use for developmental, expansion, or other purposes. Let's understand it with an example.

A company divides itself into several shares (assume 10 million shares) and has planned to sell 2.5 million shares to the general public at the price of $5. The 2.5 million shares would be listed on the

stock exchange market. Once the Stocks are listed in the Stock Markets, the investors would begin to purchase that business's stocks. Thus, if the company can sell them successfully, they can generate $50 million of capital from their stocks. The investors who have invested in the stock can hold it to generate the returns on their investment if the company or business performs well.

How Stock Market Makes Money

Now, when you know how the stock market operates, the next important question that may arise in your mind is how a stock market makes money. Basically, stock markets generate revenues from various sources, including the transaction fees, listing fees, and data generated on their platform. Here is a brief explanation of multiple sources of income and revenue for the stock exchange.

Transaction Fee Revenue

The primary source of income for stock trading markets is transaction Fees. The trading parties are required to pay the transaction fees for every trade they perform through the platform. Additionally, some trading markets such as NYSE (New York Stock Exchange) also charge a one-time registration fee and a recurring annual membership fee from the members.

Listing Fee Revenue.

A business can generate capital by listing its business on the stock exchange market. In order to list their companies on the stock exchange, the companies are required to pay the charges to the stock exchanges. Along with it, they also have to meet the eligibility criteria. During the IPO process or other follow-on offerings, the companies have to pay several charges to the stock exchange firms.

Here is an example:

At New York Stock Exchange (NYSE), there are more than 2400 companies listed. However, in 2014, around 195 Companies were listed on the New York Stock Exchange (NYSE) that generated revenue of approximately $183 Billion for NYSE. It includes 129 initial public offerings (IPO's) that raised $70.3 billion for the New York Stock Exchange (NYSE).

Data Revenue;

Real-time data, historical data, market data, summary data, and reference data constitute a large portion of the stock exchanges' revenue earnings. Basically, the stock market participants need that data for research and analysis purposes. The stock exchange participant study and analyze the data for making buying and selling decisions of the securities. Furthermore, many exchanges also provide courses and certifications on a financial topic to the stock market participant and charge for it.

The above-listed charges constitute a large portion of stock exchange earnings. Additionally, some exchange networks also charge for their trading software.

The World Largest Stock Market

The stock exchange markets are generally compared on the basis of market capitalization. The largest stock exchanges have thousands of companies listed on their network. The section explains the world's largest stock markets based on their market capitalization.

New York Stock Exchange

The New York Stock Exchange (NYSE) is at the top, with almost 2400 companies listed on this exchange. According to the reports, the NYSE has a market capitalization of $24.49 trillion as of January 2021.

NASDAQ, USA

Nasdaq is an American stock exchange with a market capitalization of $19.34 trillion as of January 2021. Nasdaq is ranked 2nd in the list of the world's most prominent stock exchanges. At Nasdaq, there are more than 3000 companies listed. The world's biggest tech giants, including Apple, Microsoft, Google, Facebook, Amazon, Tesla, and Intel, are also listed on Nasdaq.

Shanghai Stock Exchange (SSE), China

The 3rd on the list is Shanghai Stock Exchange. The Stock Exchange is located in Shanghai, China. This exchange has a market capitalization of US$ 6.5 trillion as of Jan 2021. On SSE, there are more than 1100 securities listed. Additionally, there are two different types of shares (Share A & Share B). "According to their official website, Share's "A" trades in the Chinese Yuan currency while Share's "B" trades in United States Dollars."

Honk Kong Stock Exchange (SEHK)

Hong Kong Stock Exchange is the 4th Largest Stock Exchange Market in the world. It has a combined market capitalization of US$ 6.48 trillion as of Jan 2021. According to the official website of SEHK, there are over 1100 companies listed. The top tech companies, including China Mobile and HSBC Holdings & Petro China, are also listed on Honk Kong Stock Exchange (SEHK).

Japan Stock Exchange (JPX)

Japan Stock Exchange has grown rapidly in the recent year. The exchange has a market capitalization of US$ 6.35 trillion as of Jan 202, with over 3500 companies listed. The Japanese giants, including Honda, Toyota, Mitsubishi, Suzuki, and Sony, are also listed on JPX.

24 Stock Market Participants

While you begin your investing journey, it's considerably necessary to understand the stock market participants. Therefore, in this section, we will review the participants associated with the stock market.

A stock market isn't only comprised of investors. There are numerous other players such as a stockbroker, portfolio manager, investment banker. Every participant has a special responsibility, but these roles are interconnected, helping to run the market effectively.

Stockbroker;

Stockbroker act as a Middleman who buys and sells securities on behalf of their Clients or Investors. They are also called Financial Advisor or Registered Representative. The Broker act as an Intermediate between the client and Stock Exchange for selling and buying the securities according to the direction provided by the Investor. Furthermore, Stockbrokers have in-depth knowledge about the market, and they also offer advice on buying and selling to the clients. However, the charges commission for providing their services.

Portfolio Manager;

Portfolio Managers are professionals who are responsible for managing the securities of their clients. The Portfolio Manager is responsible for making the buying and selling decisions by getting recommendations from the Analysts and Financial Experts. Additionally, they implement the trading strategies and manage the securities' day-to-day trading on behalf of their clients.

The portfolio manager is a highly experienced investor with financial background. The most significant benefit of hiring a Portfolio Manager is that it reduces the odds of risk as they are highly experienced.

Investment Banker

Investment Bankers are a part of Financial Institutions. The Investment Banker is responsible for generating capital or funds for the business, companies, or government.

The Investment Banker assists Businesses or Companies who want to take their companies to the public through the process of Initial Public Offering (IPO). They take care of the listing process of a business. Additionally, an investment banker can save a client time and money by identifying the risks associated with a particular project before a company moves forward.

Custodian & Depot Service Provider;

A Custodian is a Financial institution that is responsible for safely keeping the securities of their Clients while reducing the risk of getting them lost or stolen. The custodian may hold stocks or other assets in electronic or physical form.

Market Maker

A Market Maker is a firm or individual who facilitates the trading of shares by posting bid and ask prices. Along with it, The Market Makers are also responsible for managing and maintaining the inventory of securities.

Here it come to the end of the list. In this chapter, the main focus was to introduce the market participant and their responsibilities.

Active Trading & The Common Strategies

Active trading is the act of buying or selling securities for generating profits from price movements. The primary purpose is to generate profits by holding the shares for a shorter trend. Traders & Investors employ different strategies such as Position trading strategy or swing trading strategy to raise their earnings. Below are the details about the four common active trading strategies.

Day Trading

Day Trading is a widely famous active trading strategy. While executing the day trading strategy, the traders buy and sell the securities within the same day. At the end of the day, traders sell the securities with either profit or loss. The Day trading strategy was executed by the experts and professionals. However, electronic trading has opened up this practice to beginners too.

There are numerous technical indicators that can be employed to make buying and selling decisions. However, the most common indicator used for day trading is MACD (Moving Average Convergence Divergence), the Relative Strength Index, and the Stochastic Oscillator.

Swing Trading

Swing trading strategy is based on holding the position for longer than a single day. The traders can hold the securities for few days to several weeks to generate the profits from the investment. The trading style is ideal for those occupied with 9 to 5 jobs as they don't have to review the technical indicators daily. But to make a successful buying or selling decision, one should have to study the market for few hours.

Swing traders tend to use trading strategies such as trend trading, counter-trend trading, momentum, and breakout trading.

Position Trading

Position Trading involves keeping a position for a more extended period. Traders who execute position trading strategy don't consult with the daily fluctuation as they buy securities to keep them for a longer trend that can be a Week, Months, or years. The strategy is a great way to raise profits in the long run but not forget it can be a risky investment.

Swing Trading

Swing trading strategy is based on holding the position for longer than a single day. The traders can hold the securities for few days to several weeks to generate the profits from the investment. The trading style is ideal for those occupied with 9 to 5 jobs as they don't have to review the technical indicators daily. But to make a successful buying or selling decision, one should have to study the market for few hours.

Swing traders tend to use trading strategies such as trend trading, counter-trend trading, momentum, and breakout trading.

Position Trading

Position Trading involves keeping a position for a more extended period. Traders who execute position trading strategy don't consult with the daily fluctuation as they buy securities to keep them for a longer trend that can be a Week, Months, or years. The strategy is a great way to raise profits in the long run but not forget it can be a risky investment.

Scappling Strategy

A scappling Trading strategy is the shortest one. While executing scappling strategy, the traders keep the position or hold the stocks for seconds or minutes at most. In simple words, scalp trading strategy is about making lots of trade in a short time while generating small profits. Since the level of profits per trade is small, scalpers look for more liquid markets to increase the frequency of their trades.

31 Beginning Your Trading Journey

Millions of investors and traders try their luck in the stock market, but only a few of them succeed in raising their capital. This is just because they haven't set their investing goals, or they don't have any strategy that needs to be executed. However, if one takes an adequate time in laying out the goal and deciding the strategy, it's possible to be on the way to increase one's odds of success. Therefore, this chapter mainly focuses on beginning your trading journey.

Figure Out Your Investment Goal

While you have decided to start investing, the first and foremost thing you should do is figuring out the investment goal. By laying out the goals, you would be able to stay focused on your plans. The best way to figure out your investing goal is by asking yourself why you want to invest, whether you're saving for retirement or you want to support whatever company you're investing in.

While you are figuring out an investment goal, ensure that the goal you set is SMART. It stands for specific, measurable, attainable, relevant, and time-oriented.

Specific: What is the purpose of the goal?
Measurable; What is my indicator of progress?
Achievable; What are the resources that I need to achieve my goal?
Relevant. Why am I doing this?
Time-oriented. What is the deadline?

You can have a goal as simple as "I am planning to earn $2000 within a year from my investment to buy a brand-new car" or one that's a little more complicated like, "I want to generate 40% profits on my actual investment within a year."

Opening a Brokerage Account

Once you have figured out your investment goals, the next step is opening your brokerage account. While you are choosing the stockbroker, there are a few things that you need to consider that include:

- How much is the cost per trade?
- How much minimum initial investment is required
- Proper Asset Allocation Guidance
- Easy-to-use website or smartphone application.
- Direct Investment Advice
- Do they give access to investment research?
- What Are Investment Options Available?
- Do they have ethical investing options?

- How much interest is offered on uninvested funds?
- Customer Support

These are some of the few things that you need to research before choosing a brokerage. It may be pretty tricky for you to find the right broker. However, you can check out the reviews about them to identify whether it suits you or not.

Buying & Selling of Stocks.

Buying & Selling Stocks is the most crucial step in investing your capital in the Stock Market. There are numerous things that need to be considered when you are planning to buy or stocks. There are numerous indicators that can help you make a decision that shall bring favorable outcomes for you. A few indicators are:

- Stochastic oscillator
- Bollinger Bands
- MACD
- Average directional movement index
- Relative strength index
- On-balance volume
- Moving Average

By analyzing these technical indicators for each stock, one can identify whether it's time to buy it or sell. We shall discuss some of these indicators in detail in the upcoming chapter.

Beginning Your Trading Journey

Additionally, The Stock Prices can also move with numerous non-technical factors that are as follows.
- Government Policies.
- Economical Condition
- Technological changes
- Natural disasters/extreme weather fluctuations
- The performance of the business or organization in the past few years.

These are the few things that you need to consider while making buying and selling decisions. By doing market research and studying the patterns, it's become relatively easier to make significant decisions that can raise your capital. It may take time to see some favorable outcome but keeping yourself focused would surely help you make the right buying and selling decisions.

Additionally, The Stock Prices can also move with numerous non-technical factors that are as follows.
- Government Policies.
- Economical Condition
- Technological changes
- Natural disasters/extreme weather fluctuations
- The performance of the business or organization in the past few years.

These are the few things that you need to consider while making buying and selling decisions. By doing market research and studying the patterns, it's become relatively easier to make significant decisions that can raise your capital. It may take time to see some favorable outcome but keeping yourself focused would surely help you make the right buying and selling decisions.

36. The Indicators

Despite the uncertain fluctuations, the stock market would usually follow a general trend, which can be predicted using the relevant tools. The stock exchange is a big business, and people would put up huge money in order to earn profits. It is full of foreign investors who have all the available techniques to make the best profits in the long run. Before you get into the business yourself, it is better to learn how the market works rather than buying shares on the assumption, which would possibly turn out wrong. The workings of the market are simple to predict using the latest indicators, which are designed for specific purposes. The indicators come with a 75% accuracy in guiding whether to make a purchase or not or simply predict whether the share would rise or fall. In this section, we will be discussing several of the most important indicators that may be helpful for you in making a decision.

Moving Averages

It is one of the most common indicators and is simple to understand. If you are new, start by ignoring the word "Moving" and concentrate only on "Average." Average refers to the mean of all values over a period of time; moving refers to the fluctuations that arise on a daily basis or simply as constantly changing. The basic Moving average graph is made to smoothen the movements of changes in value. It would often be represented by a straight line with lesser fluctuation that follows the main candle pattern.

Candlesticks are a method of evaluating the fluctuations in share value for a day. The more expansive bar illustrates the value of shares in the market over the day and its comparison with the past day, while the stick shows the maximum and least value the share was traded at. The pattern is complex than it, but for our purpose of working with moving averages, the explanation is good enough to move ahead.

One of the popular indicators that make use of Moving Averages is the MACD or the moving average convergence divergence; the basic diagram involves a zero-axis, above which all positive values exist while the bars below it indicate negative values.

38

The zero-axis is aligned at a value that is the average price of the share over a certain period. When the candles move above the zero axes, it indicates that the share has a positive rise in its value; the bars move like histogram, where the middle bar indicates the greatest increase. While the bars alongside it refer to positive movements, as soon as the bars turn negative and start rising in the negative region, it indicates that the share's value is decreasing, the same pattern of rising to a peak and then falling is also followed like the positive region.

To help you make a decision when the bars are in the positive region, the indication refers that the share value would rise over time, so you must buy it, while if it falls in the negative region, it indicates that the share price is going to go down and it is time to sell.

The MACD histogram is supported by two curves, which are colored in red and blue for better representation. The red line indicates the moving average for the last 12 days, while the blue one shows the moving average for 26 days. The blue line is called the signal line, which predicts how the share might react in the near future. Once the blue line cuts the red line from below, it is an indication that the moving average or the share price is going to rise, so a buy signal is communicated.

On the other hand, when the red line cuts the blue line, it means that the moving average and the share price are going to decline; this communicates a sell signal. The curve and the histogram are to be used together for better predictions. If the blue line cuts the red line in the negative half, it means that the share price is about to rise, and the purchase must be made. Similarly, if the red line cuts the blue line in the positive half, the share prices are predicted to go down, and the sale should be made.

Relative Strength Index

RSI is concerned with the selling and purchases of shares in a market; it can have a value from 0-100, where values ranging from 30-70 are usual for shares to play in. It shows the capital power of shares and the investment allotted to them. When a share is purchased extensively, its RSI value may rise, alongside its share price, which means the company has more funds invested in it; similarly, if a share is oversold, the RSI would fall, alongside the share price, which means investors are withdrawing their funds from the company which reduces its overall worth.

An RSI value of 30 or below indicates that the share is being oversold and the price of the share is shaping down; it is an instant where the share may bounce upwards, and the prices may rise. On the other hand, A RSI value greater or equal to 70 indicates that the share is being overbought and the price is already peaking; when the RSI value is at the stage, a bounce is due, and investors anticipate the prices to fall.

For you to make decisions, you can wait for the RSI to drop below 30 before purchasing the shares as it has high chances that it may rise and have little chances of falling back. Similarly, if you analyze a

share closing to the 70 benchmarks, ensure that you don't purchase the share as it has little chances of rising and more chances of falling further. Experts, however, have suggested to buy a share close to the 50 mark and selling it within the region as it is a period of certainty. RSI is an easier indicator to understand for newer investors as the representation is easier to elaborate, and the curve moment is reliable to predict the future movements of the markets.

The On-Balance Volume

The volume itself is an important indicator and determines the pattern of investments flowing the market. The volume shows the number of shares traded in an economy; the more the number of shares traded, the greater the volume and publicity of the company. Bigger companies tend to have an overall volume of more than 1 million on regular days. However, on-balance volume measures a little more than just volume; it is a curve drawn out of normal patterns of volume traded. The point of the curves is calculated by adding the sales of the day subtracted by the sales of the last day. If the shares traded today are more than the previous day, the curve takes an upward turn; on the other hand, if the shares traded have had a downfall, the curve will slope downwards.

The indicator is difficult to understand on a let alone basis; however, once the share price is kept alongside it, the on-balance volume could prove effective in predicting the exact future. For instance, if the share prices are rising, and the volume line is trending upwards, then there is a fair chance that the share price would keep on rising; however, if the volume line turns flat with the prices rising, it can be the instant where the prices have peaked and

may turn downwards. In cases of falling share price, if the volume line is rising, it means that the share would keep on falling as more volume traded means that there are suppliers who are willing to supply at the low price; however, as soon as the line turns flat or starts falling, we can anticipate the share price to have hit the lowest, and there are possible chances of a bounce back.

The indicator can be challenging to get-on with for new investors as they might often be misled amongst multiple companies. Some lesser-known firms might have a sudden upsurge and down-surge in volume, which would give mixed signals; because the number of shares traded is low, the increase won't create a significant impact for more than some days. We would suggest using the indicators for well-known companies that are amongst the top 20 volume leaders so that your investment stays safe.

It is the end of the section; we are hopeful that the three indicators are effective for you to make good earnings from the stock market. The MACD, RSI, and on-balance Volume should be paid due heed, and purchase should only be made when the MACD agrees with either the RSI or on-balance Volume; if the MACD doesn't agree or give a suspicious feeling, it is better not to make a

purchase or sale. The other two indicators are important too, but MACD should be your first priority.

Now we will further discuss the tips about getting started with the stock market so that you have all the required skills before you invest your hard-earned money.

45 Tips to Make a Successful Investment

Now you have in-depth knowledge about stocks, and you may ready to invest your capital in the stock exchange market. But before you step down, there are a few things that you should remember to make a successful investment in the stock exchange while reducing the odds of losses.

There are several things that need to consider while investing, such as diversifying the investment, creating emergency funds, etc. By following these tips and experts' advice, you would surely be able to get excellent returns on your investment.

Diversify Your Investment

The best approach to reduce the odds of losses is by diversifying your investment. Often, investors or traders commit a mistake by investing their entire capital into a single business, which leads to losses for them if the company doesn't perform as of their expectation. That's why financial experts' advice for diversifying your investment into several sectors, for instance. If you plan to invest $2000 in Stocks Market, then the best approach would be diversifying it. You can invest diversify 25% in the Automotive Sector and 25% in the Technology Sector, while the remaining can be invested into other sectors such as Medical, Energy, etc. In this way, the odds of the losses would be dramatically reduced.

46

Don't Be Impatience;

The young or newbie traders are impatient, as they want to see the outcomes quickly, which isn't the right mindset. When the traders are driven by Impatience, they aren't able to make the right decisions.

Businesses take time to implement the new strategies. For example, if a company plans to expand its business. Then the process of expansion is time-consuming. It may take several months to years for the execution of their plan. But the investors will buy shares of the stock and then immediately expect the shares to act in their best interest. That is the wrong mindset. You need to be realistic about it is means you need to keep your expectations natural with regard to the timeline for portfolio growth and returns.

Neglect the Averaging Down Technique.

One of the most significant blunders beginners make is executing the averaging down technique. Generally, investors or traders implement averaging down technique when they have purchased stock at a higher price, but after some time, the stock has lost its value. In such situations, the traders will purchase an additional share at a lower price to cover the cost of loss.

For Example. If an investor has purchased 100 shares of a Company at a price of $5. But the price has dropped to $4. Now, the Investor will buy additional shares at the price of $4 to lower their losses. The strategy may seem beneficial, but in fact, the investors or traders are investing their capital into a share that has already lost its value. Therefore, most financial experts suggest not to execute the Averaging Down Technique.

Implementing Strategy from Untrustworthy Sources

While investing your capital in a company or business, you must ensure that you aren't following news from untrustworthy sources. There are too many people who would call them experts, and they would be willing to tell their opinions and strategies to you. All you need to do is staying away from these so-called experts as they would only give you advice that may not be right.

The most significant thing that you need to do is focusing on the right information that comes from trustworthy sources. Once you are able to identify the experts in the field, take their suggestions and combine them with your research to make the decision that brings some favorable outcomes for you. However, one thing that young investors or traders should remember is that if someone is being featured for an Interview by top media, then it doesn't make him the expert. So, make sure that you don't follow any so-called expert.

Create an Emergency Fund Before Investing Your Principal Amount

Most of the financial experts recommend creating an emergency fund before investing the capital. This is just because investing includes various sorts of risk. Therefore, the best approach is to set some funds for emergencies. Additionally, there are numerous benefits of the Emergency funds, such as the Investor wouldn't have to apply for a Mortgage. Thus you don't have to pay any interest or wait for a long time to get some capital. So, ensure to create emergency funds. In case your decisions don't go in the right direction, or you face some financial hardship, the emergency funds would surely cover your expenses.

Evaluate the Risk Involved in It

Investment isn't only about profit. It includes some degree of risk. If you decided to invest in securities such as stocks, mutual funds, then it's essential to understand it before you invest. You can even lose your entire capital by making a single wrong decision. This is just because the price of stock always varies.

The reward for taking a risk by investing has excellent potential. If you have invested for the long-term, you are likely to make big bucks. However, you will have to invest carefully and don't take the unnecessary risk that shall put a bad impact on your investment portfolio.

1 2	3 4 5	6 7 8	9 10
Very Low Risk For Investor	Low To Medium-risk Investor	Medium To High-risk Investor	Very High-risk Investor
Not prepared to accept any risk to money invested whatsoever.	Prepared to accept a certain level of investment risk in return for the possibility of higher investment returns over the long term.	Happy to accept a higher level of risk on investment if this results in higher investment returns. Prepared to accept some loss to investments.	Very speculative investor, willing to accept the loss of some or even all of their investment in return for the possibility of very high returns

The table explains the risk associated with each investment. The risk in investment varies on a scale of 1 to 10, where 1 is considered as the lowest risk while a risk level of 10 indicates a high-risk investment.

Tips to Make a Successful Investment

Rebalance Portfolio Time to Time

Rebalancing is the process of periodically buying and selling portions of your portfolio to maintain an original level of asset allocation. The biggest benefit of rebalancing is that it lowers the risk. Rebalancing tends to work best when done on a relatively infrequent basis.

Here's a simple example to understand the concept of rebalancing:

Jessy has $2000 to invest. She invested 50% of her capital in Stock while the remaining 50% in Mutual Funds. After some time, the stock performed well, and it could have increased the stock weighting of the portfolio to 70%. Now, the investor (Jessy) decided to sell her stock to bring her portfolio back to the original position of 50/50.

There are numerous strategies for rebalancing such as calendar-based, corridor-based, or portfolio-insurance based. Often, investors prefer calendar-based rebalancing.

Review Regularly, But Not Too Regularly

Once your investment portfolio is ready, ensure that you are making changes frequently. "Research shows that investors who watch their investments day to day tend to buy and sell too often and get poorer returns than investors who leave their money to grow for the long term."

The Market fluctuates on daily basis. Sometime, it reaches the peak and often, touches the lowest mark. If you're a long-term investor, you can just ride out these fluctuations.

Here we come to the end of the list. Investing is great way to yield great profits. However, you need to play smart and make well-informed decisions that shall bring good results for you. By following these strategies, you would surely be able to make good returns on your investment.

www.ingramcontent.com/pod-product-compliance
Lightning Source LLC
Chambersburg PA
CBHW070854220526
45466CB00005B/1998